Fused Tattoo Machines
Tattoo Machines Builders
Worldwide Collaboration

Second Edition

www.FusedTattooMachines.com

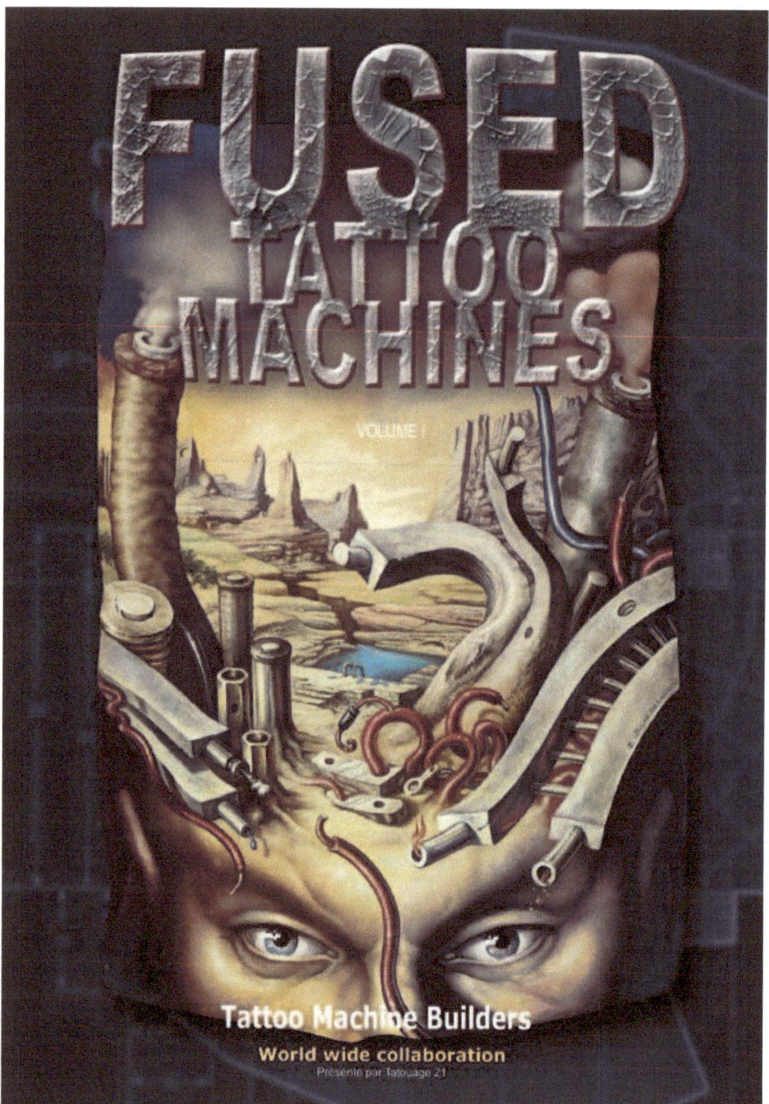

FUSED
TATTOO
MACHINES
VOLUME I
Tattoo Machine Builders
World wide collaboration
Présenté par Tatouage 21

This book was first published in a limited edition in 2011.
We have decided to republish it to keep alive the
interest in coil tattoo machines and to celebrate
the craftsmanship behind them.

Thanks

Iko

Artwork : Patrick CHAUDESAIGUES

www.FusedTattooMachines.com

Réédition / Reissue 2023 Iko, Delux Custom Editions

« Restons ce que nous avons toujours été : des gens libres.
C'est devenu suffisamment rare pour qu'on s'accroche ne serait-ce qu'à l'idée. »

« Let's stay the way we've always been : free people.
This has become sufficiently rare to stuck to the idea, whatever the cost. »

Enki BILAL, *Le sommeil du monstre*

Foreword

Builders from all over the world share their passion and come together around the project of creating tattoo machines collaboratively. Each machine is like an 'artistic masterpiece' where creative originality and technical mastery merge to give birth to a unique piece.

The Fused Tattoo Machines collection is a testament to this drive for expression and independence that characterizes free spirits.

Dano Collins and Mike Hendrix

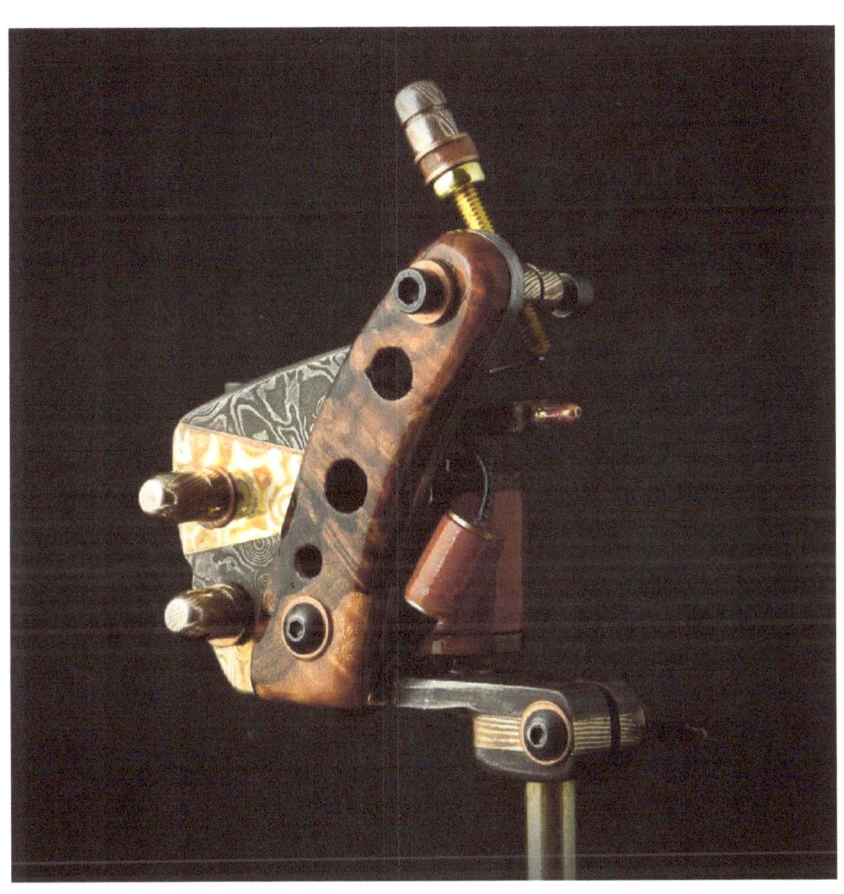

Steve Turner and Andy Bolin

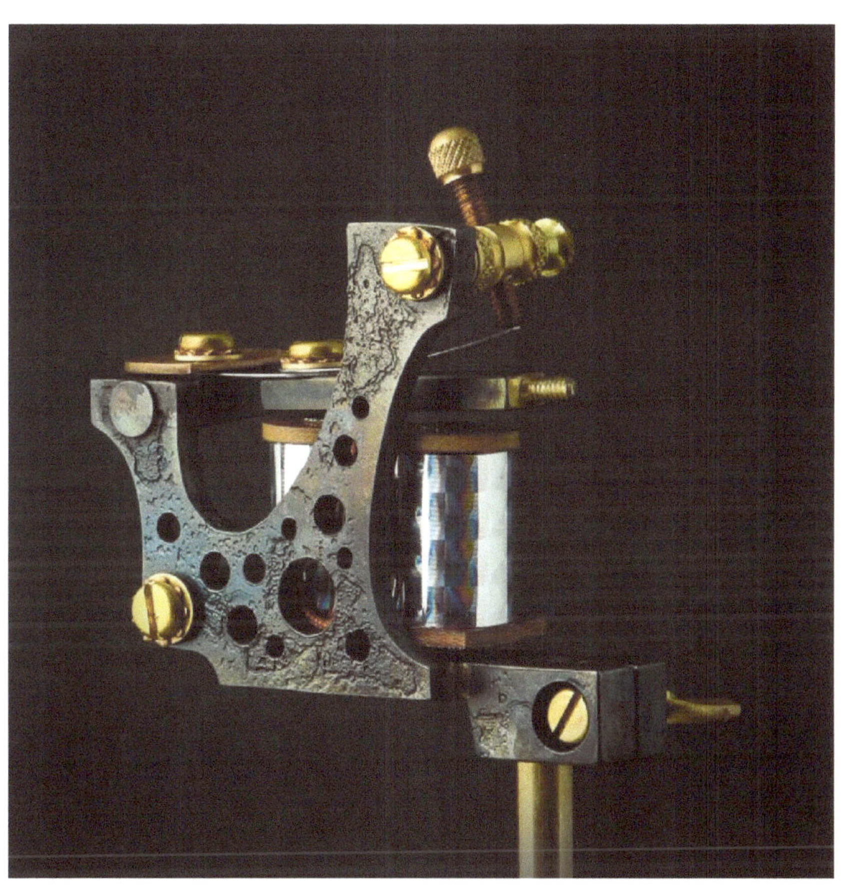

Mike Pike and Wife

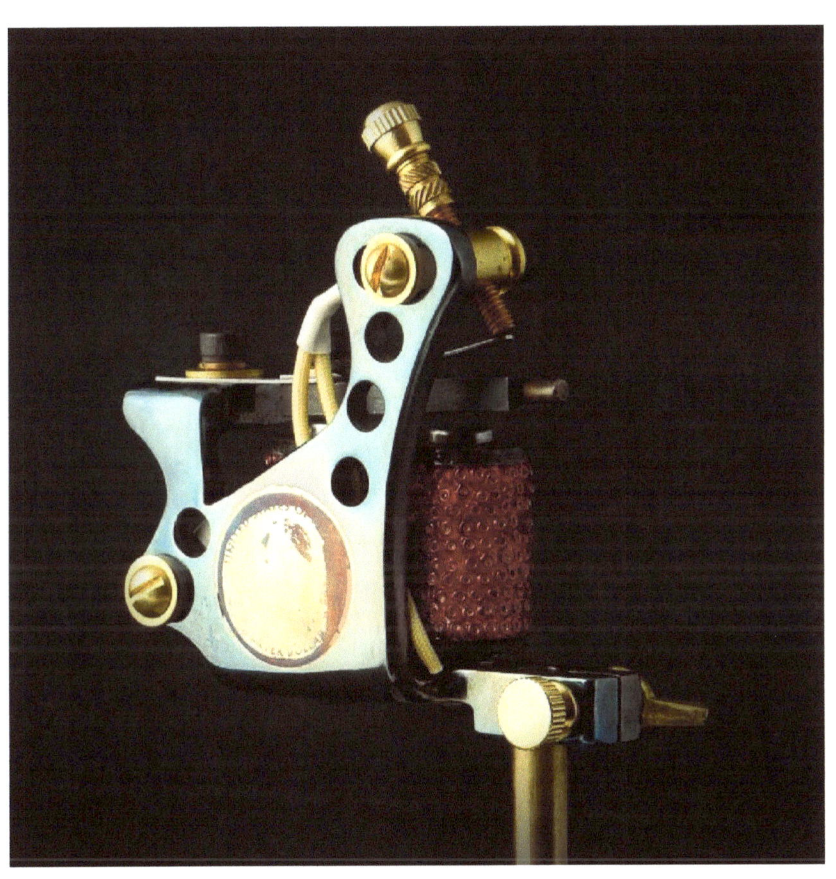

Chris Quidgeon and John Clark

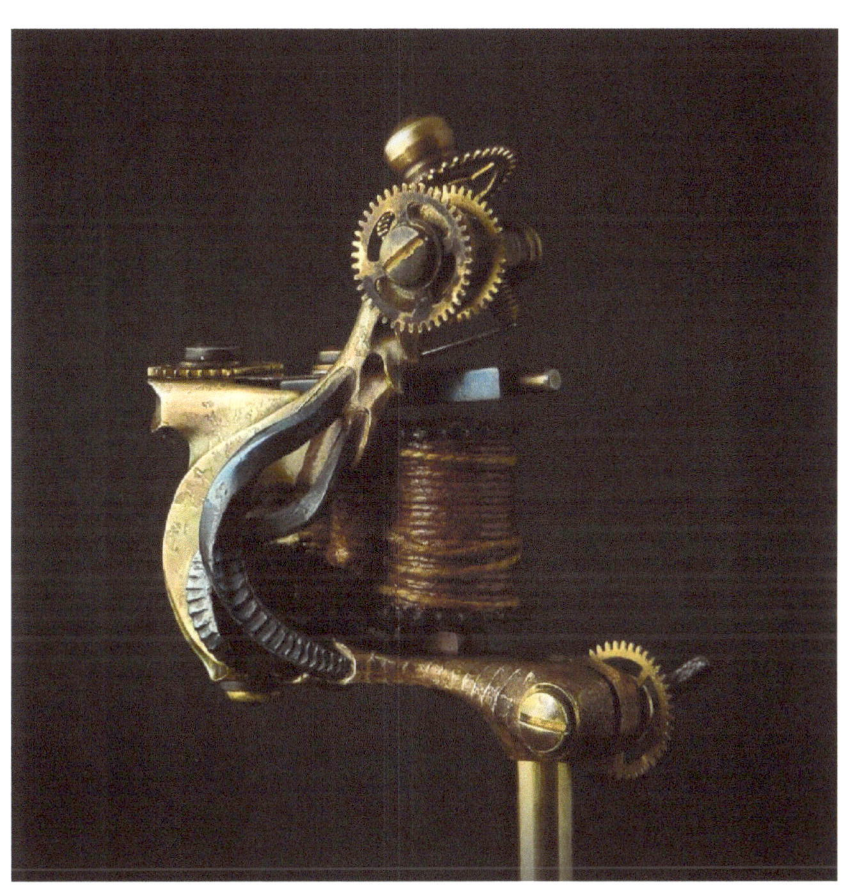

Greg DiGiacinto and Dirk Mellott

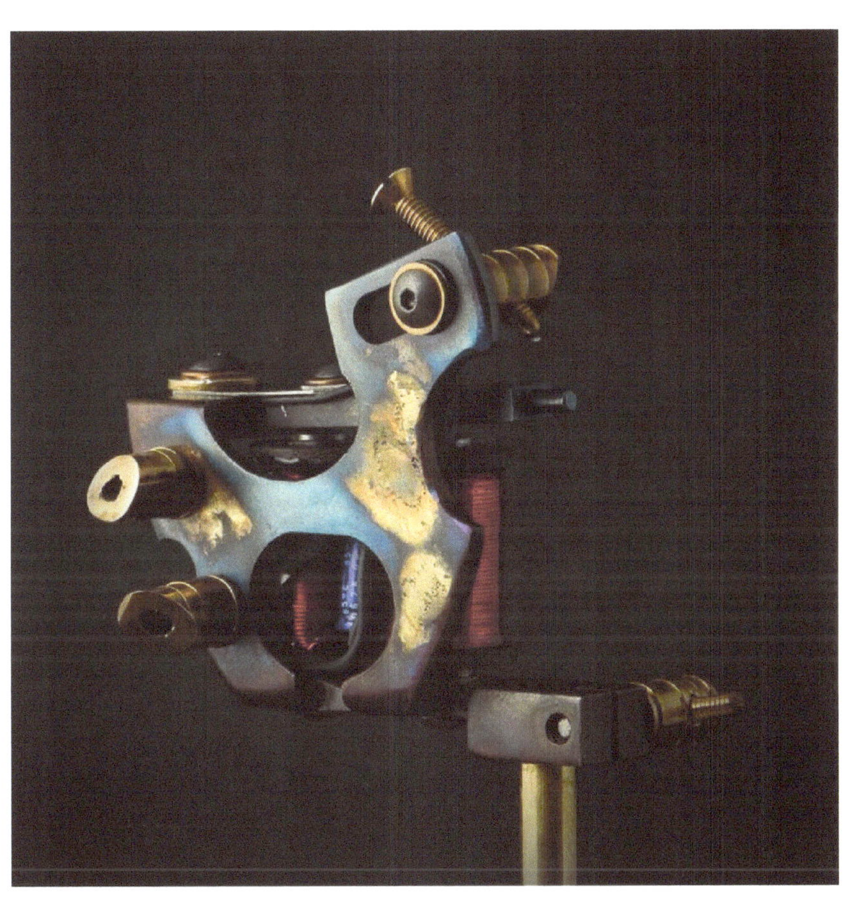

Safwan and Dan Labonté

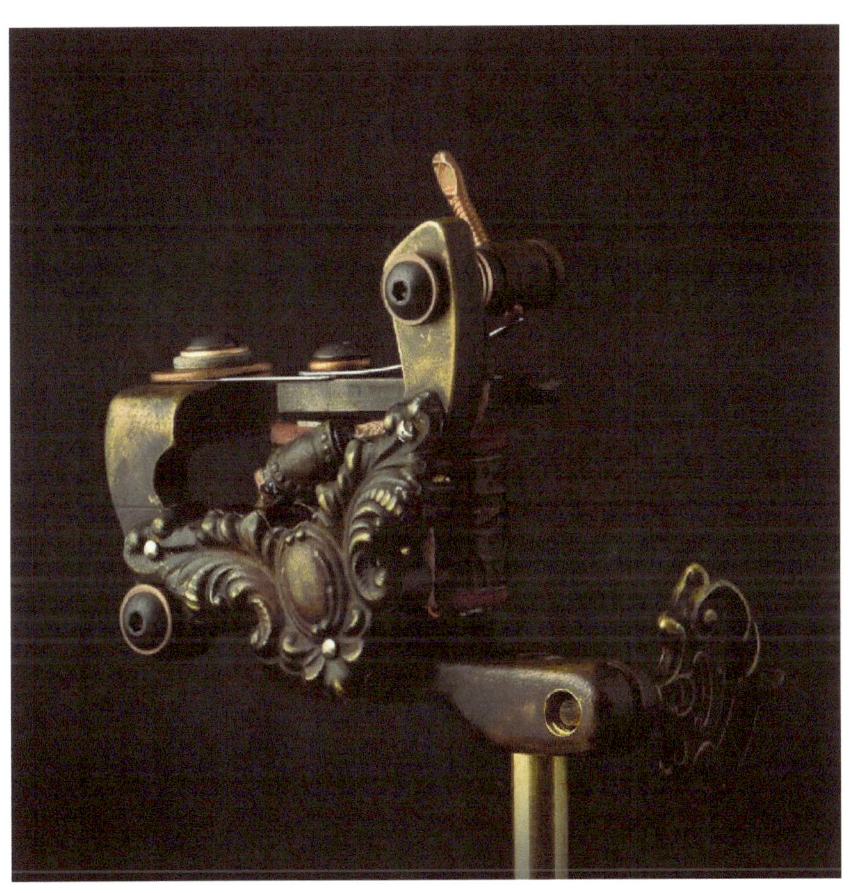

BR Irons and Austin Riley

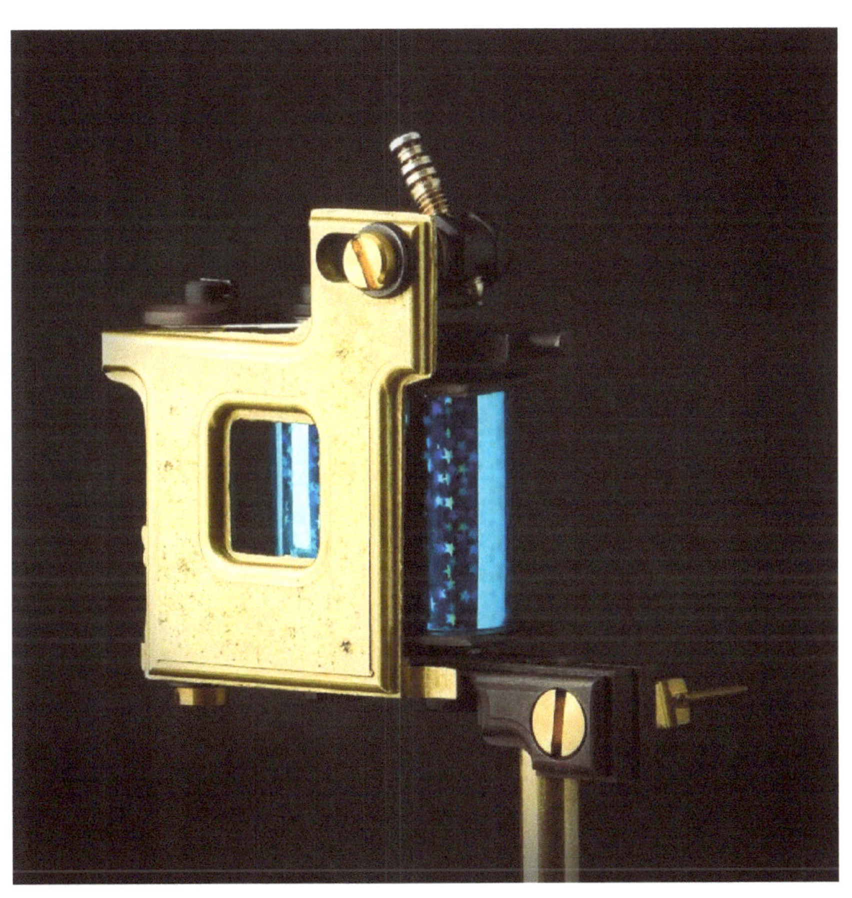

Paulo Cruzes and Dan Dringenberg

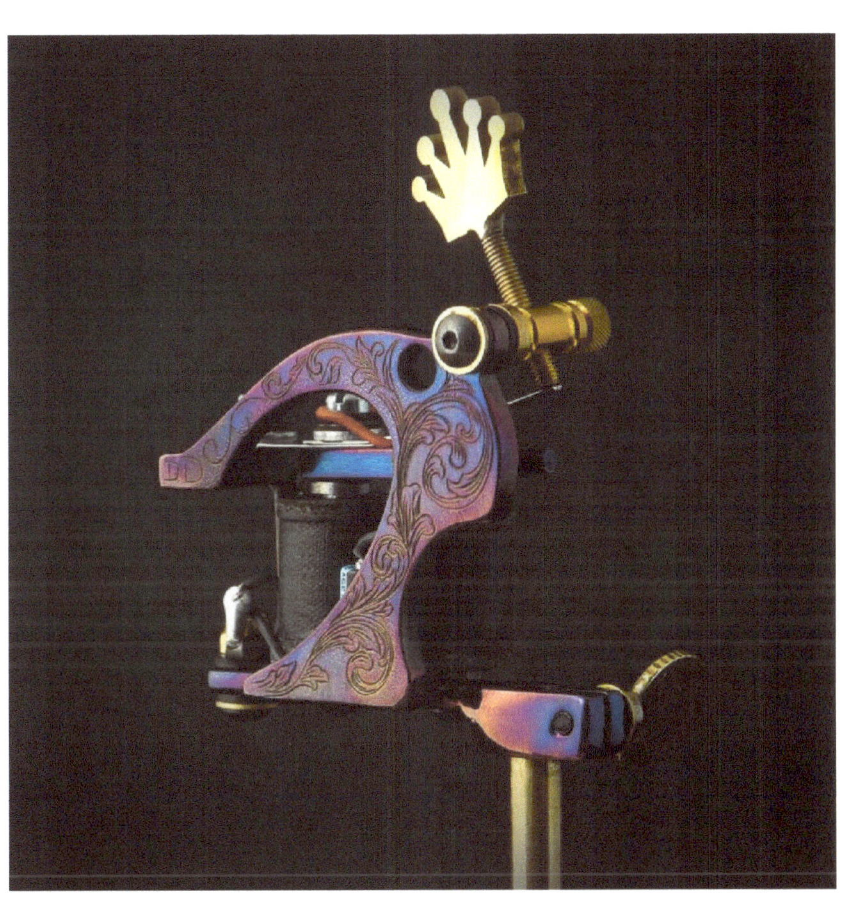

Rob Rutherford and Marv Lerning Esquire

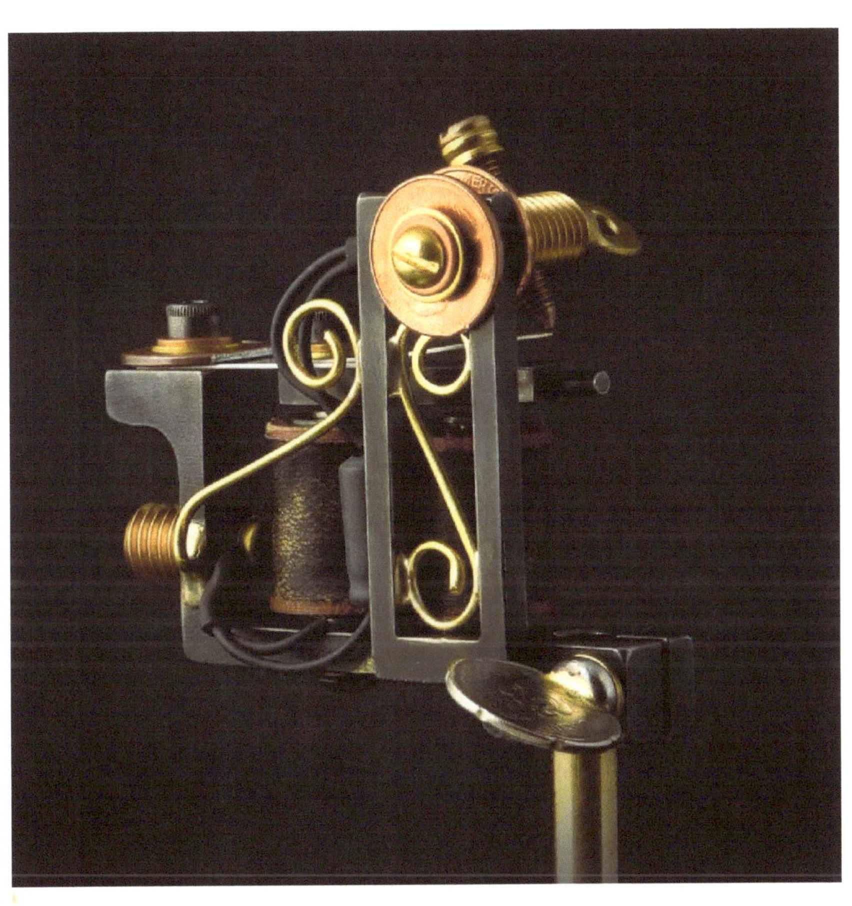

T. Massari and Dr. Blood

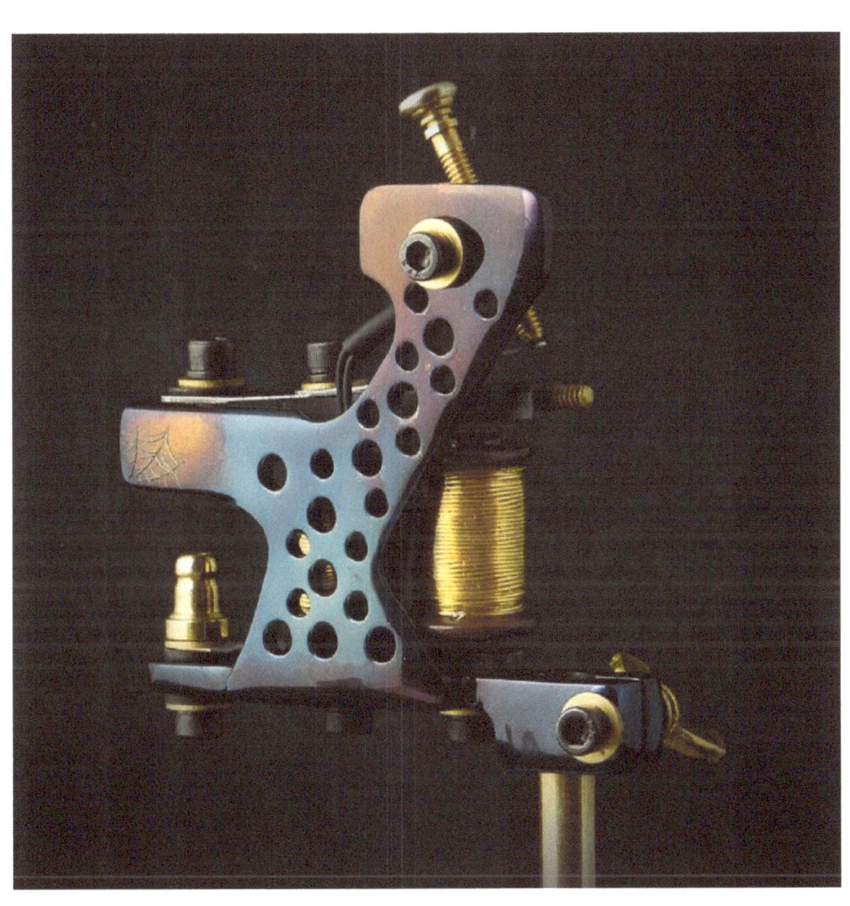

Jon Ondo and Chunk

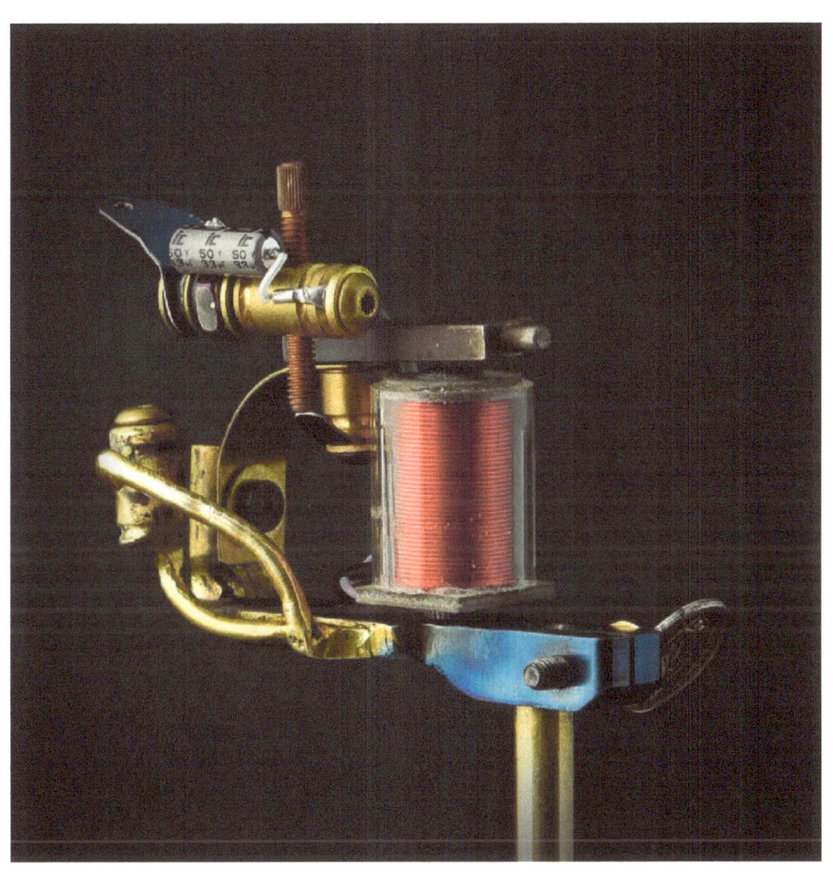

Mike Young and Jason Haney

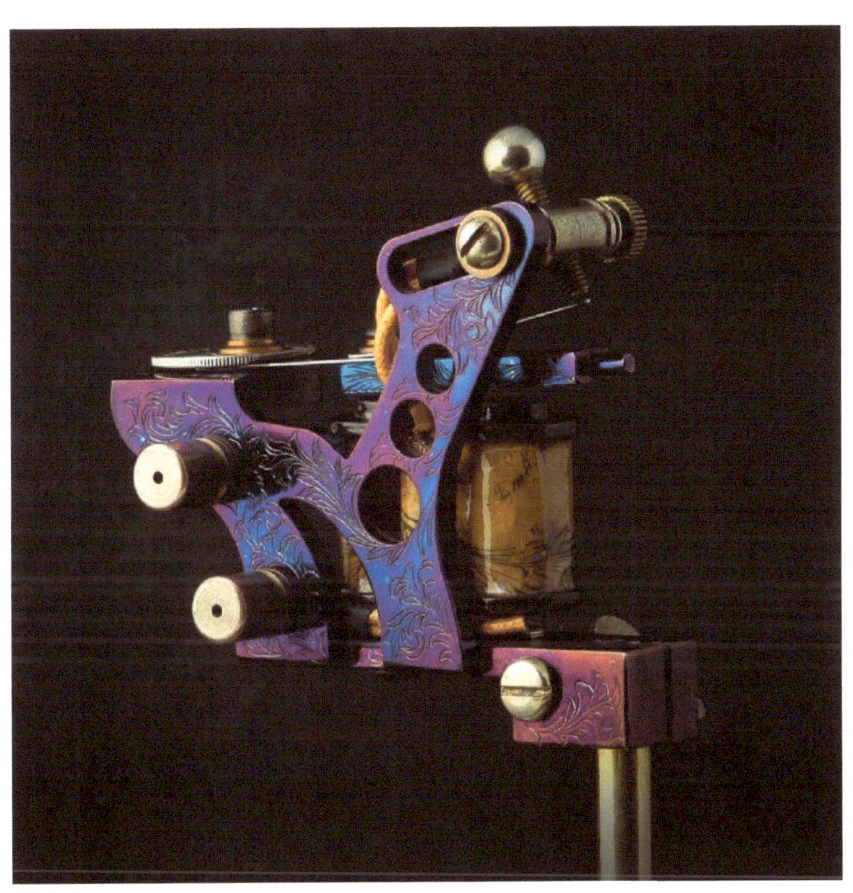

Andy Bolin and Henry Rodriguez

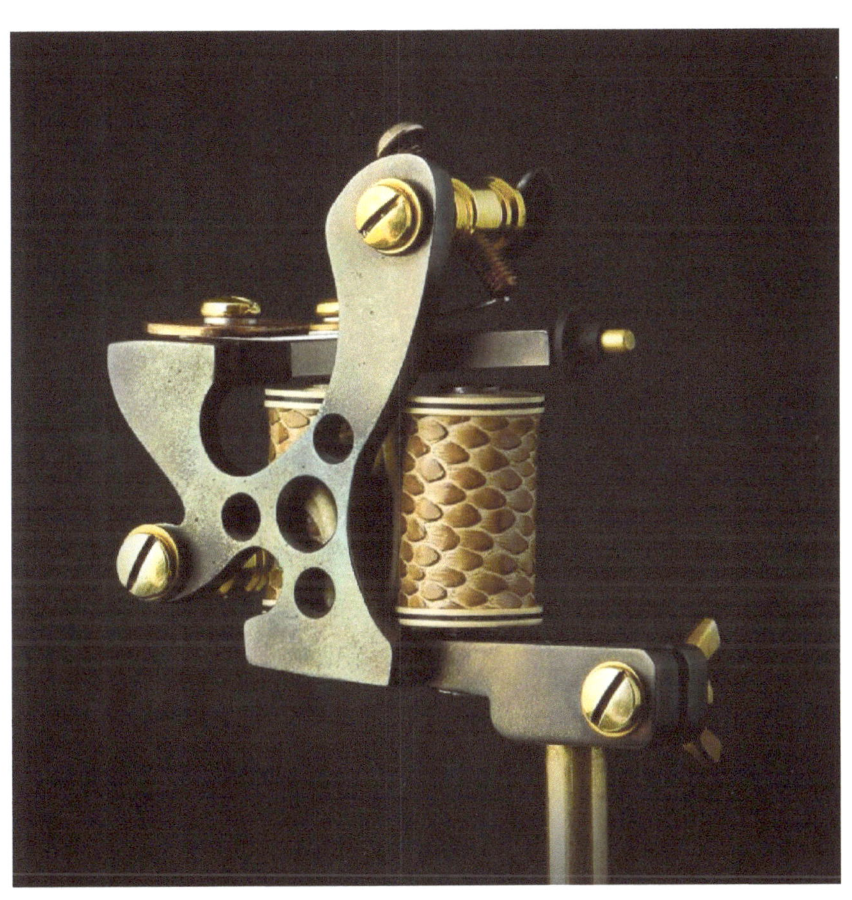

Mike Pike and Wife

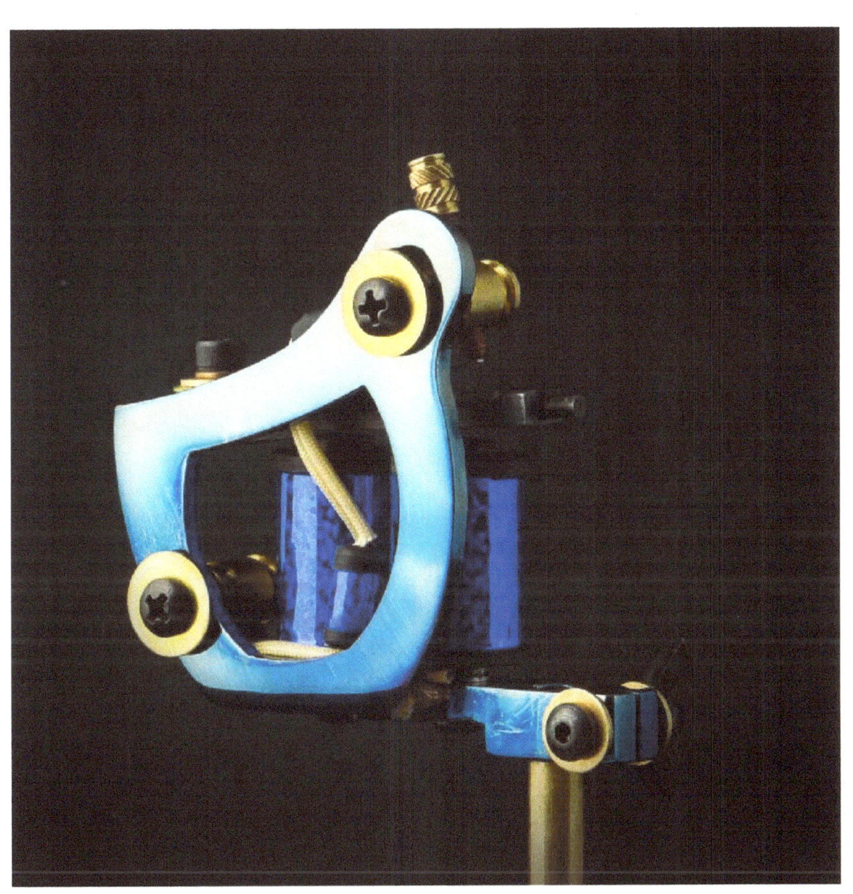

Jimmy Whitlock and Iko

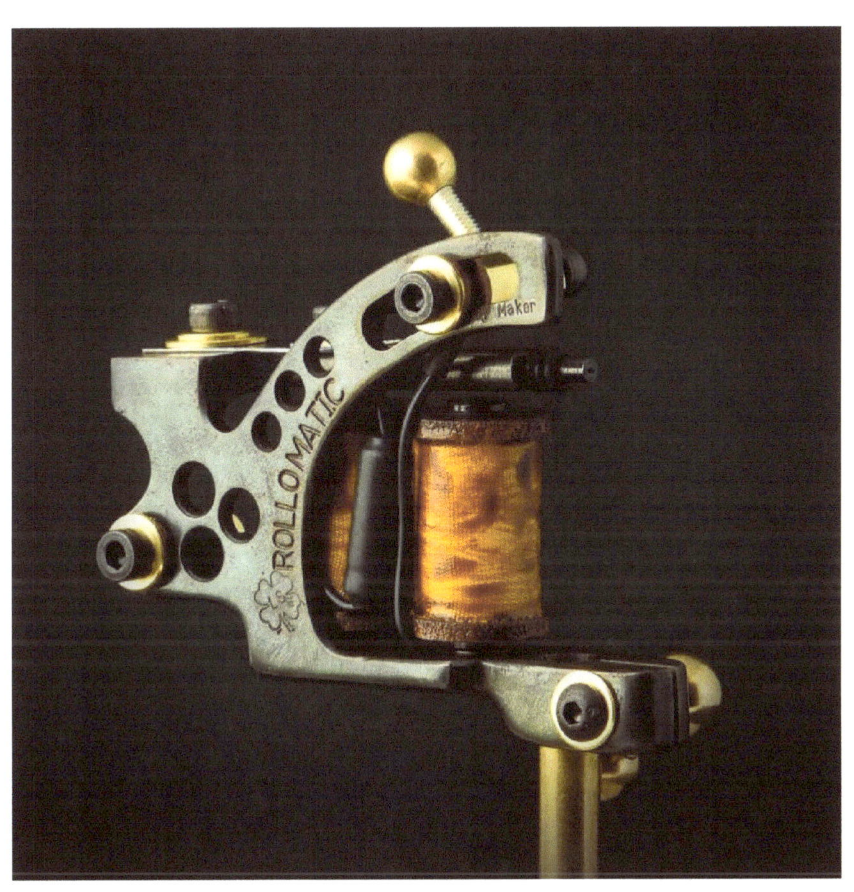
ROLLOMATIC
Maker

Toma and Nicko

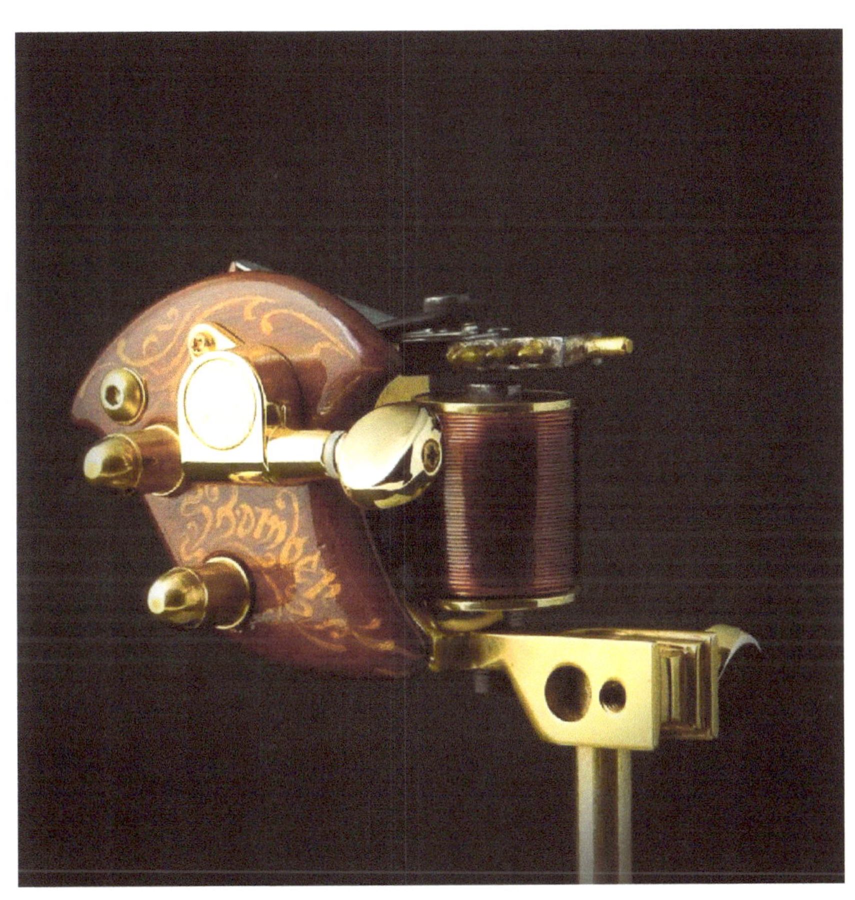

Soba and Cory Rogers

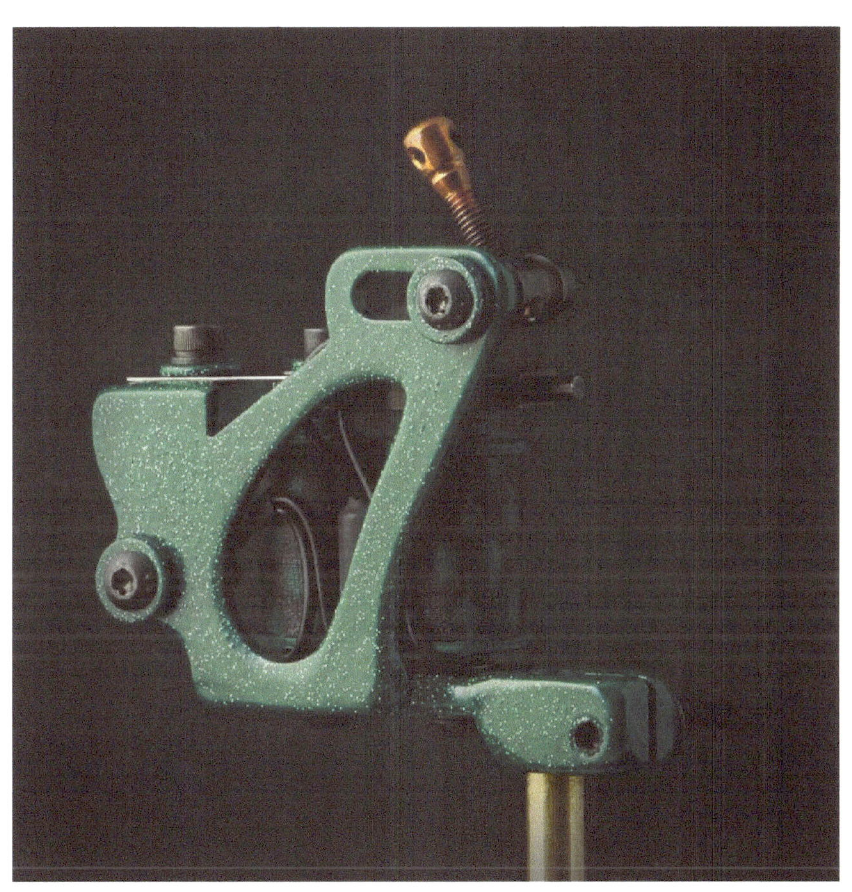

Iko and Jimmy Whitlock

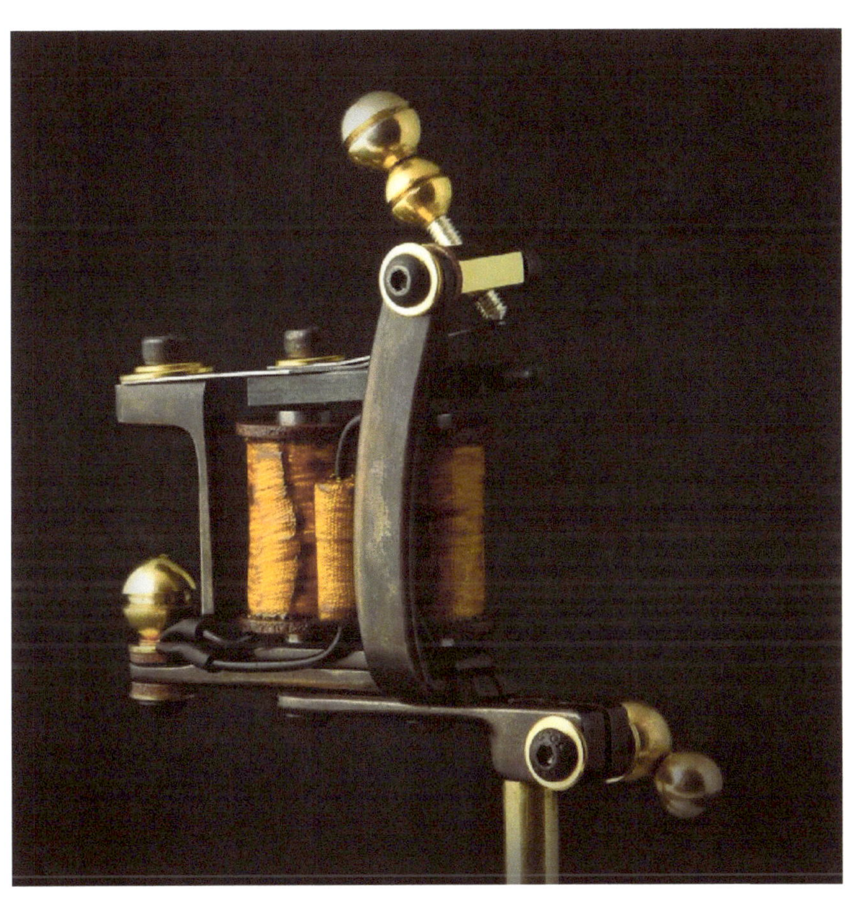

Tomas Khajl and Peter Bobek

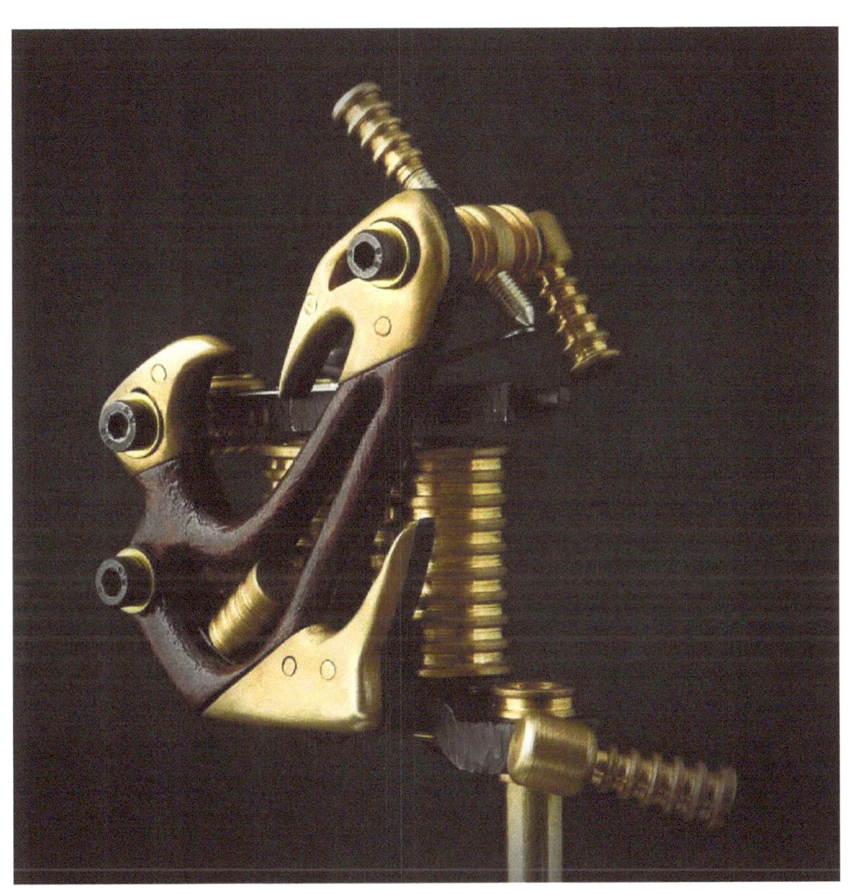

Marv Lerning Esquire and Rob Rutherford

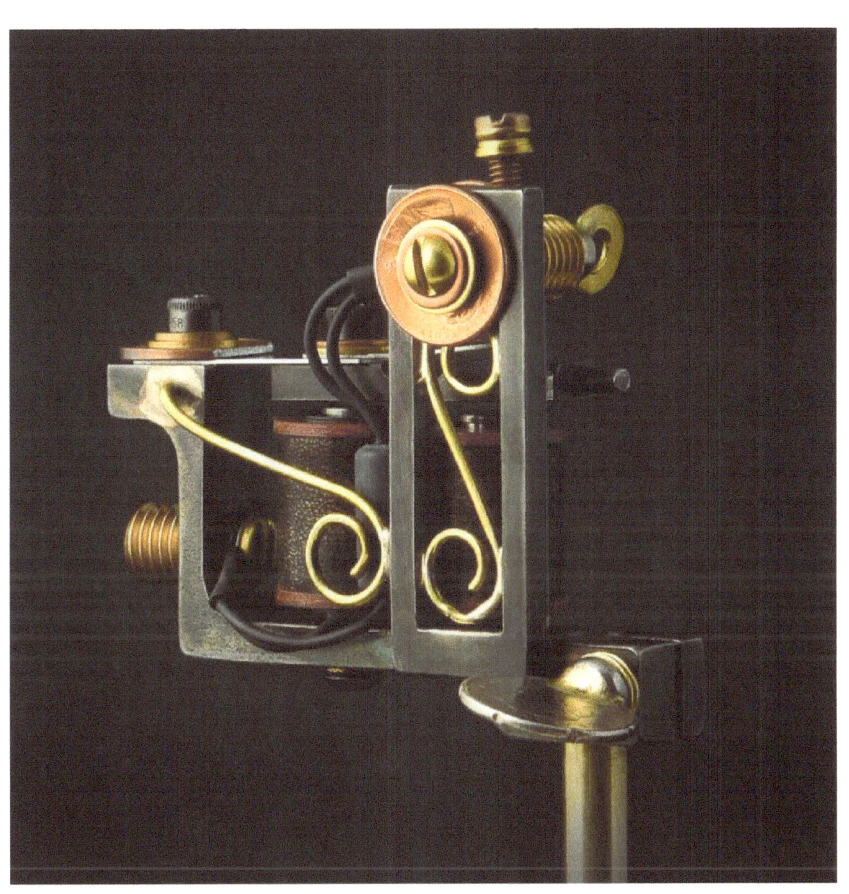

Salva and Dennis El Hombre Invisible

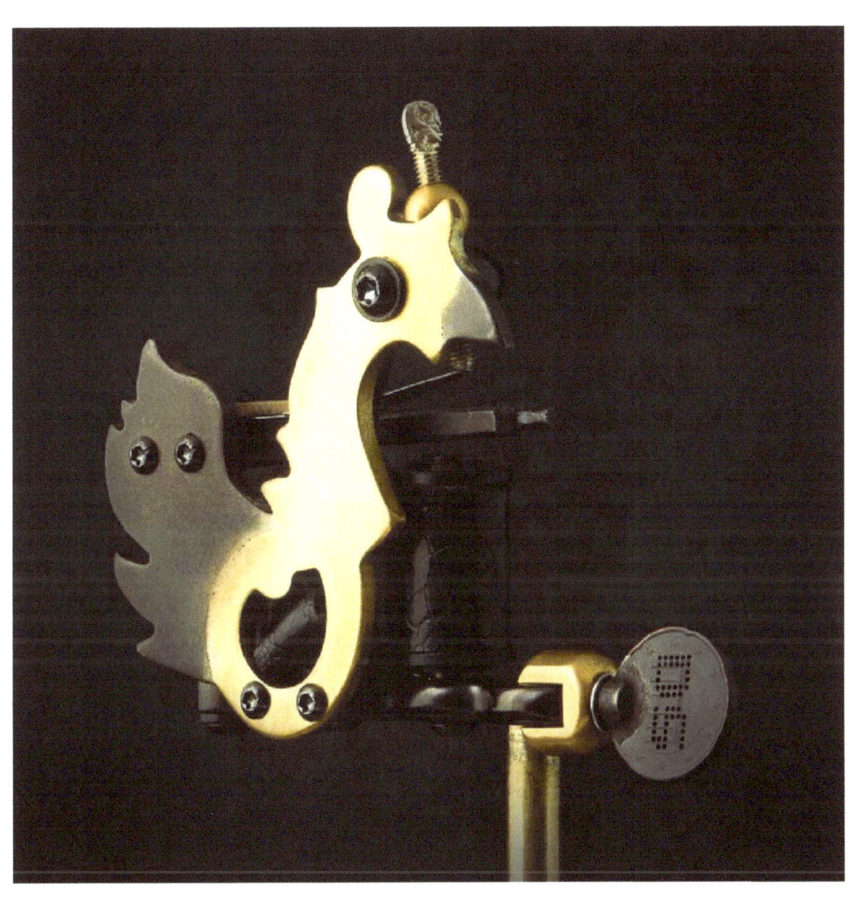

Todd Hlavaty and Joseph Mc Veigh

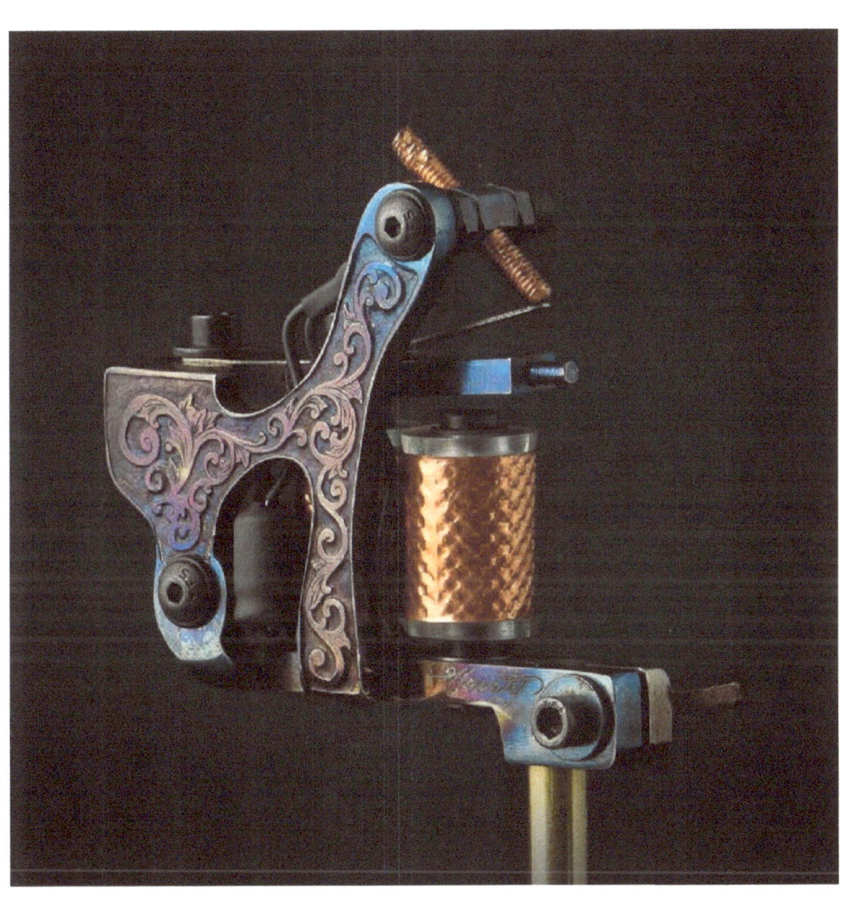

Nick Ackman and Kris Cunningham

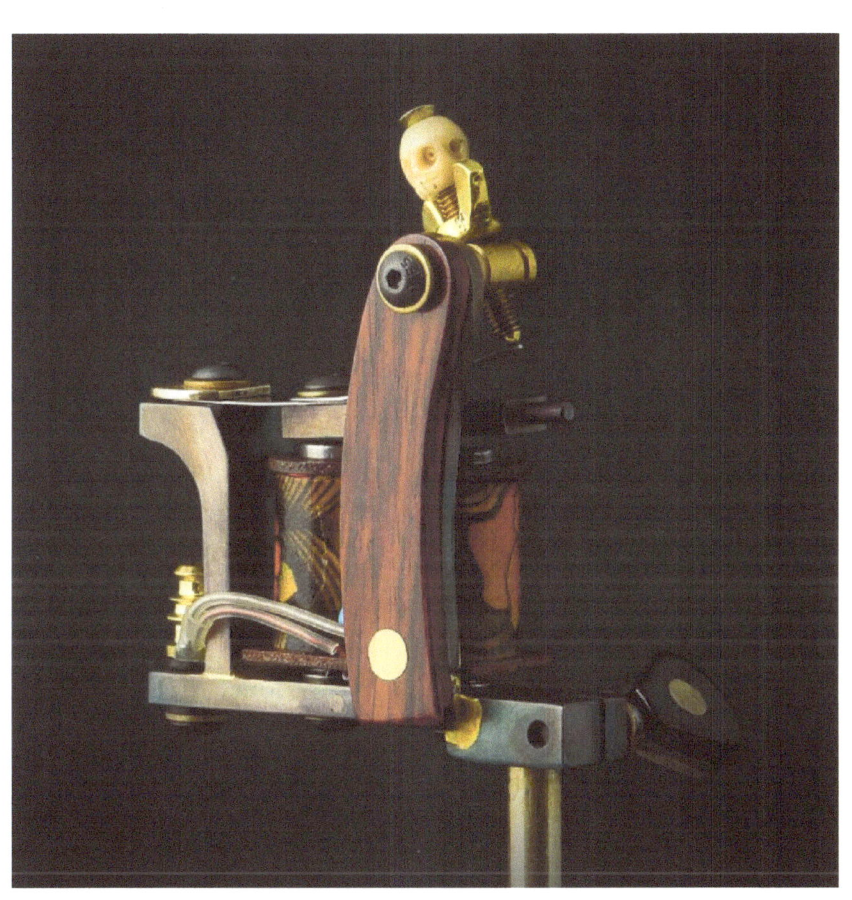

Iko and Dan Labonté

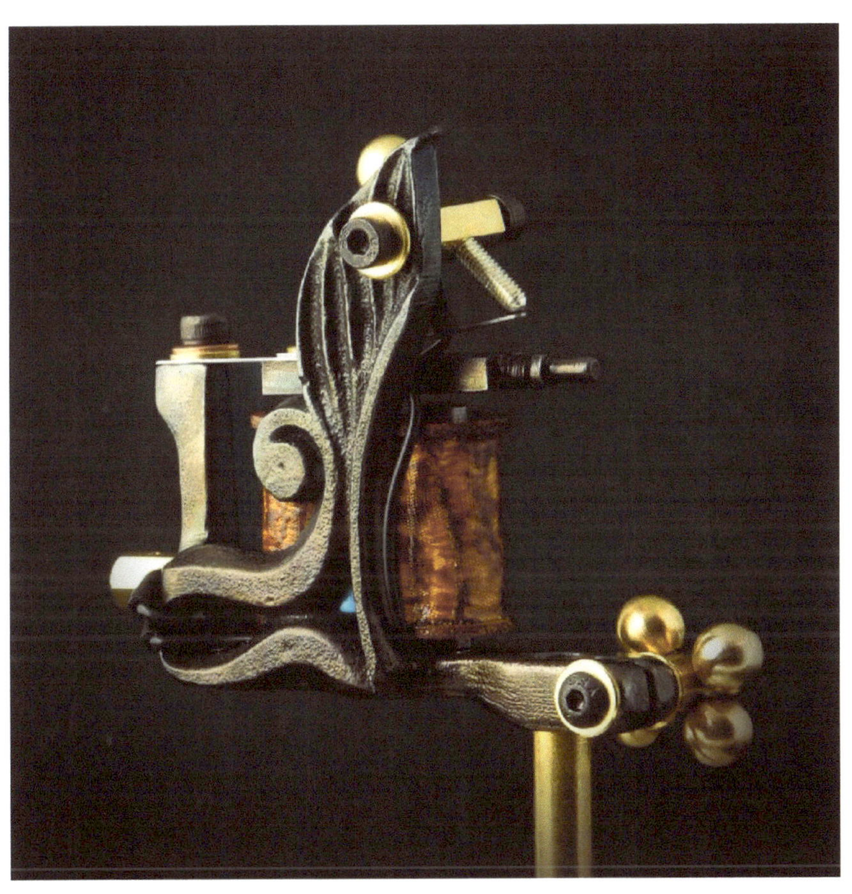

Austin Riley and BR Irons

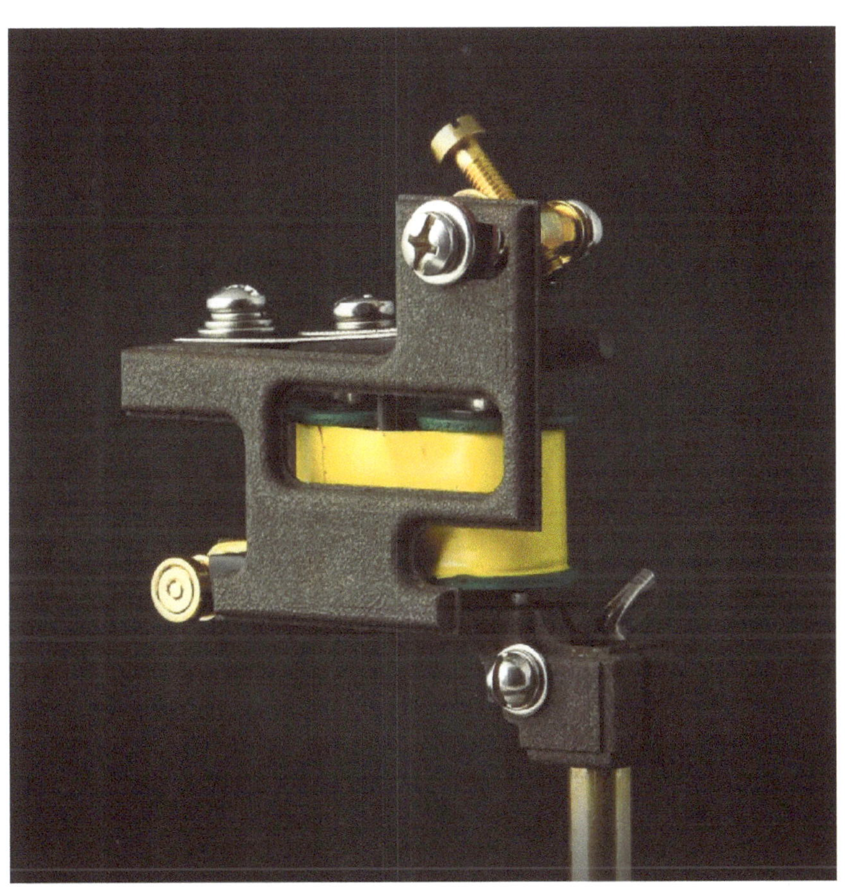

Rex Hobbs and Brian Fuentes

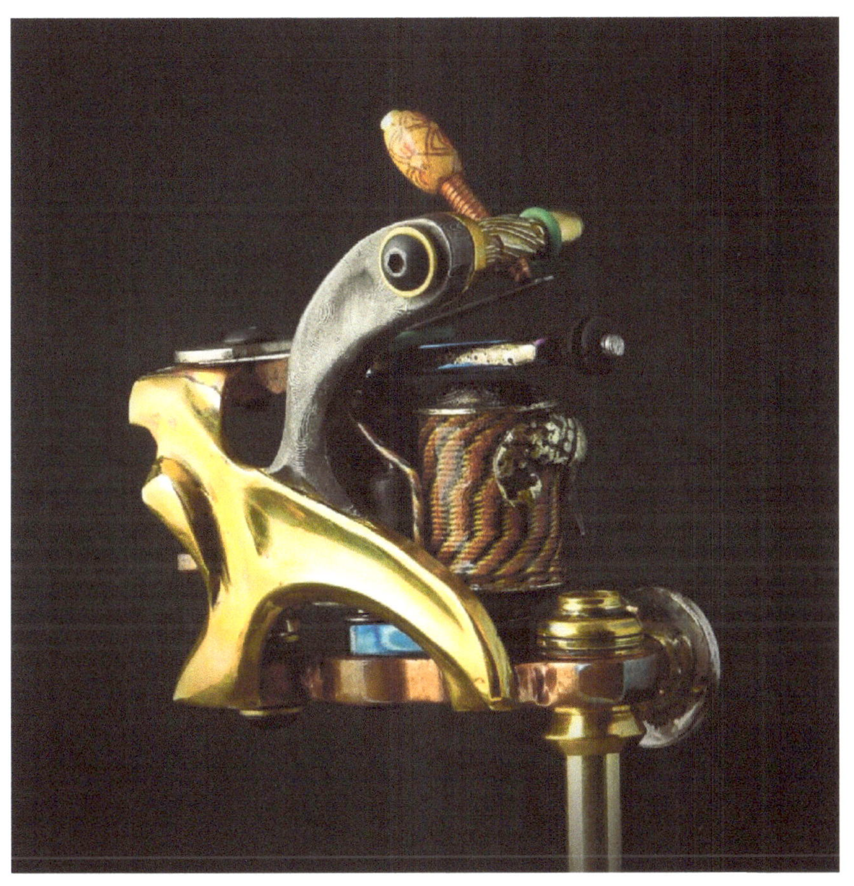

Brian Fuentes and Charles Freeland

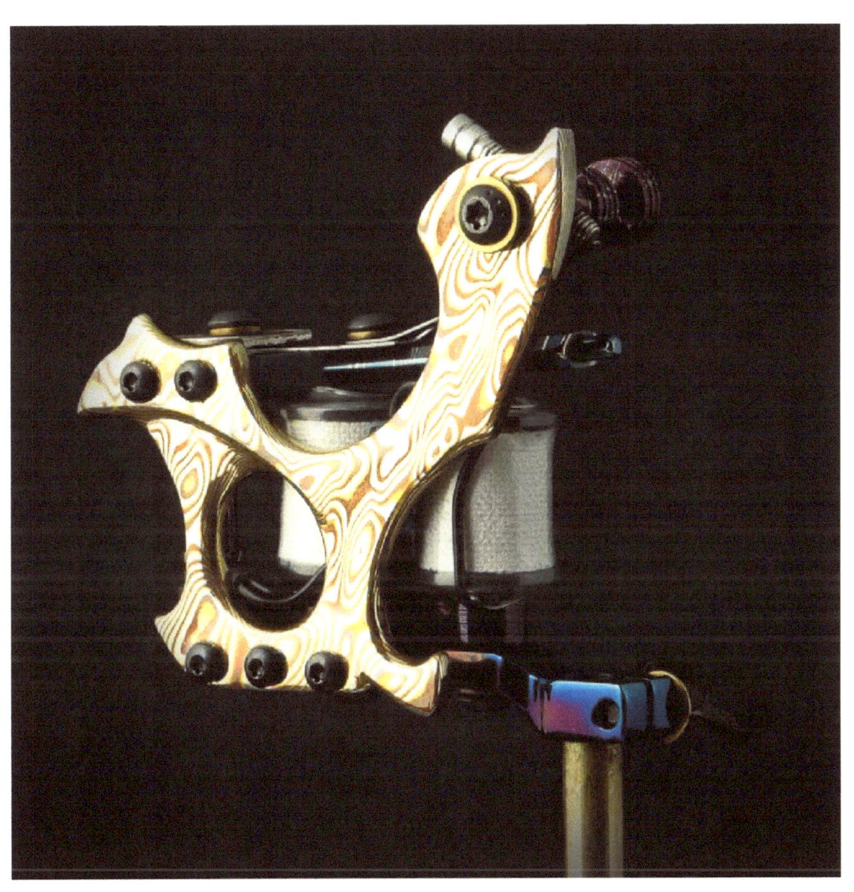

Jay Addictive and Mike Palombo

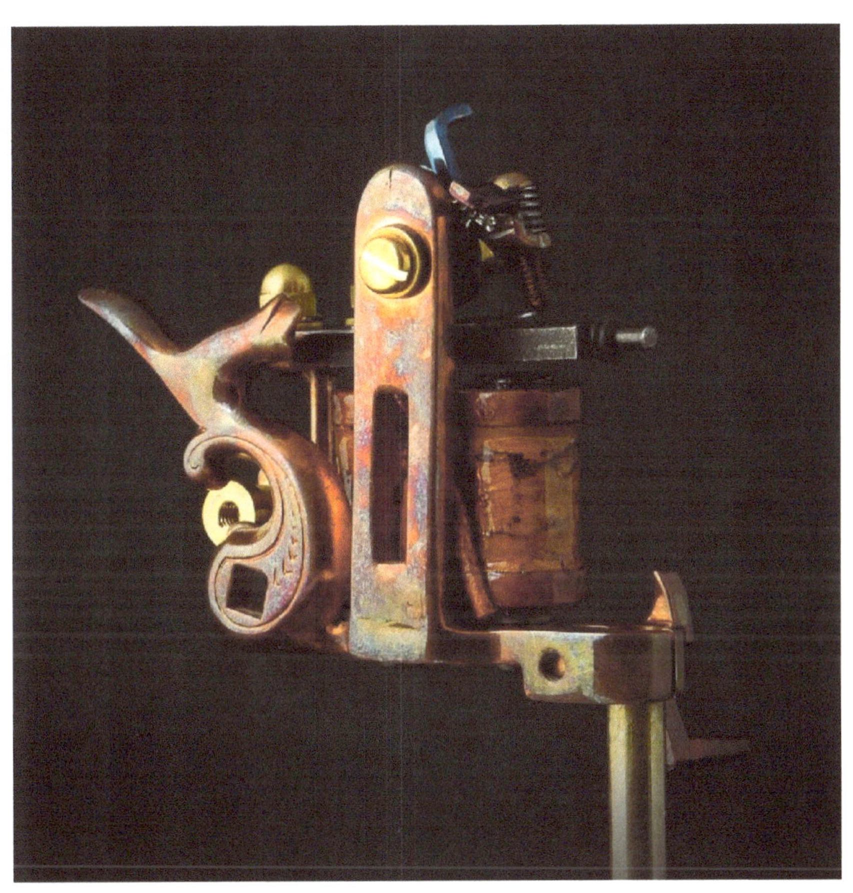

Sebastian Lutz and Bryce Stucke

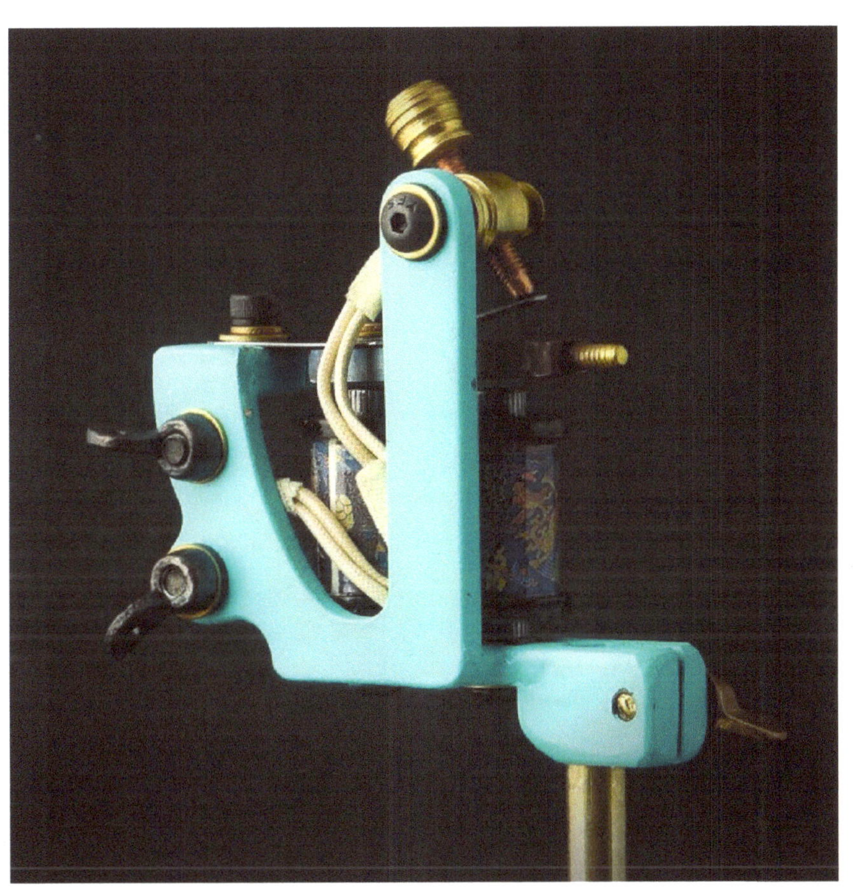

Patrick Chaudesaigues and Karl Marc

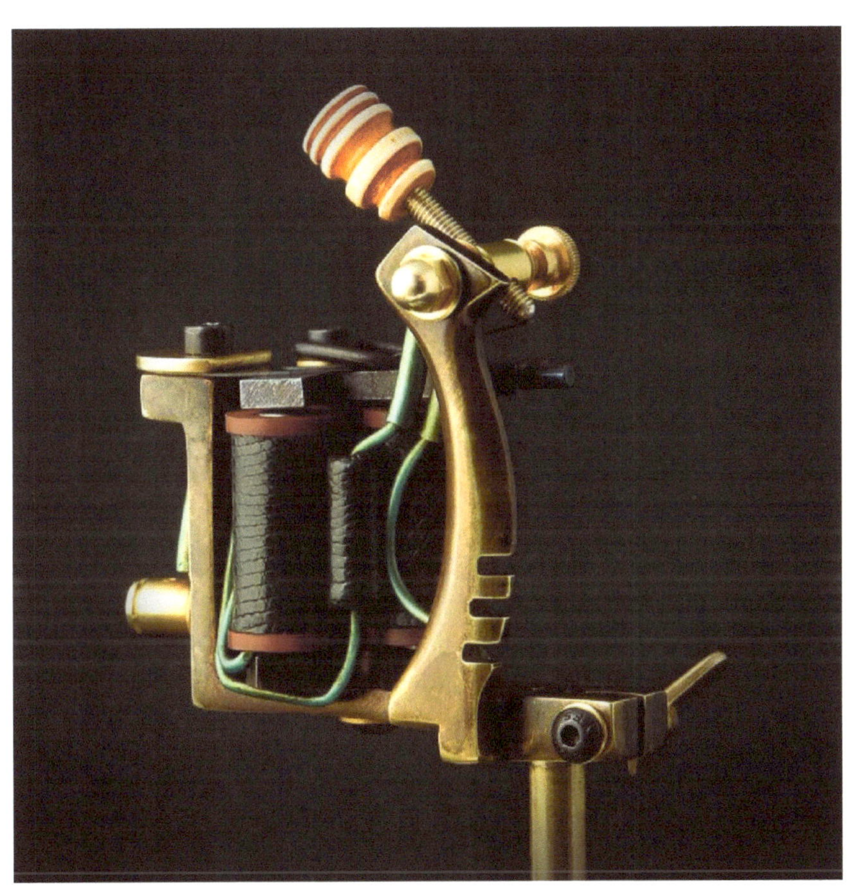

Andy Bolin and Steve Turner

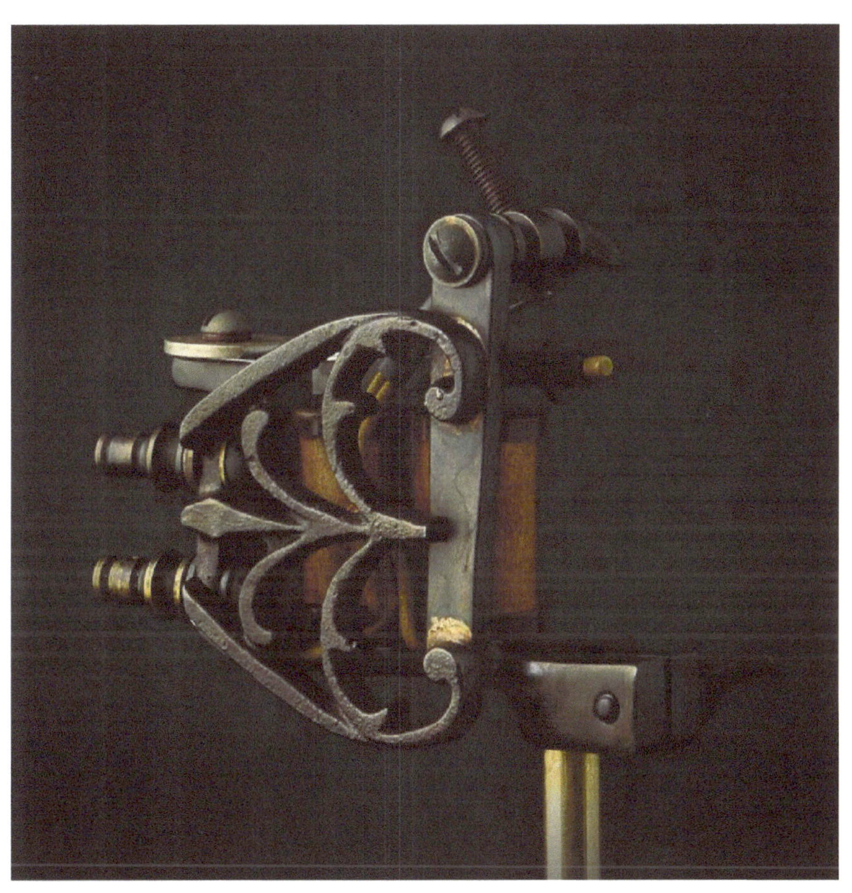

Henry Rodriguez and Andy Bolin

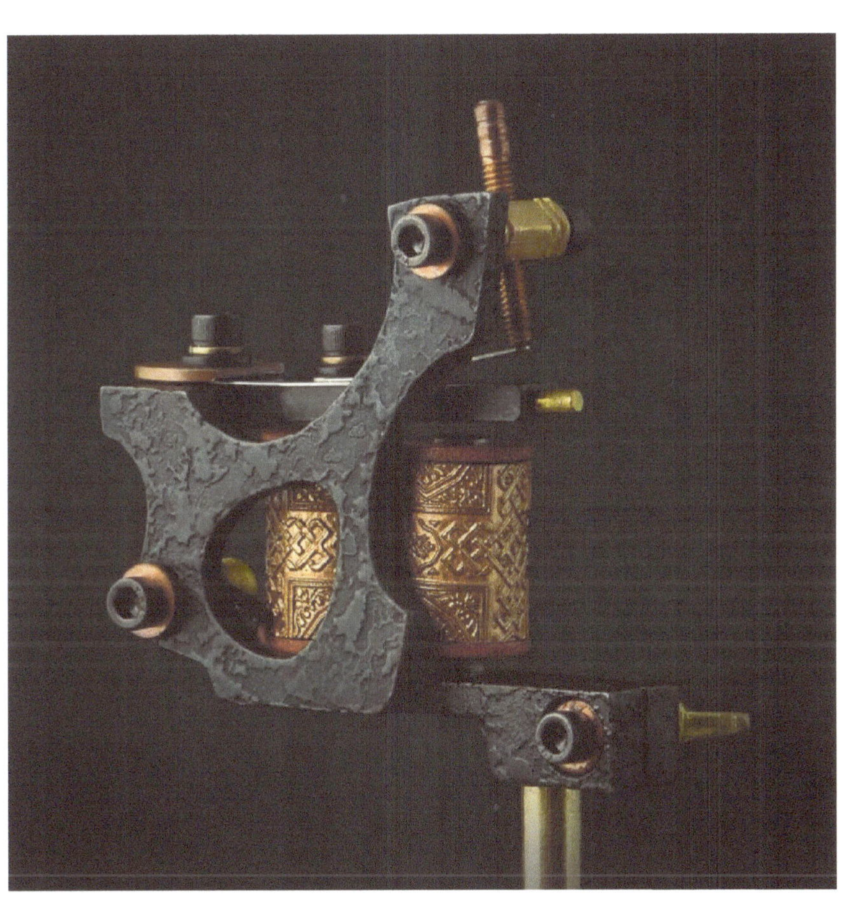

Bruno Kea and Chris Bonobo

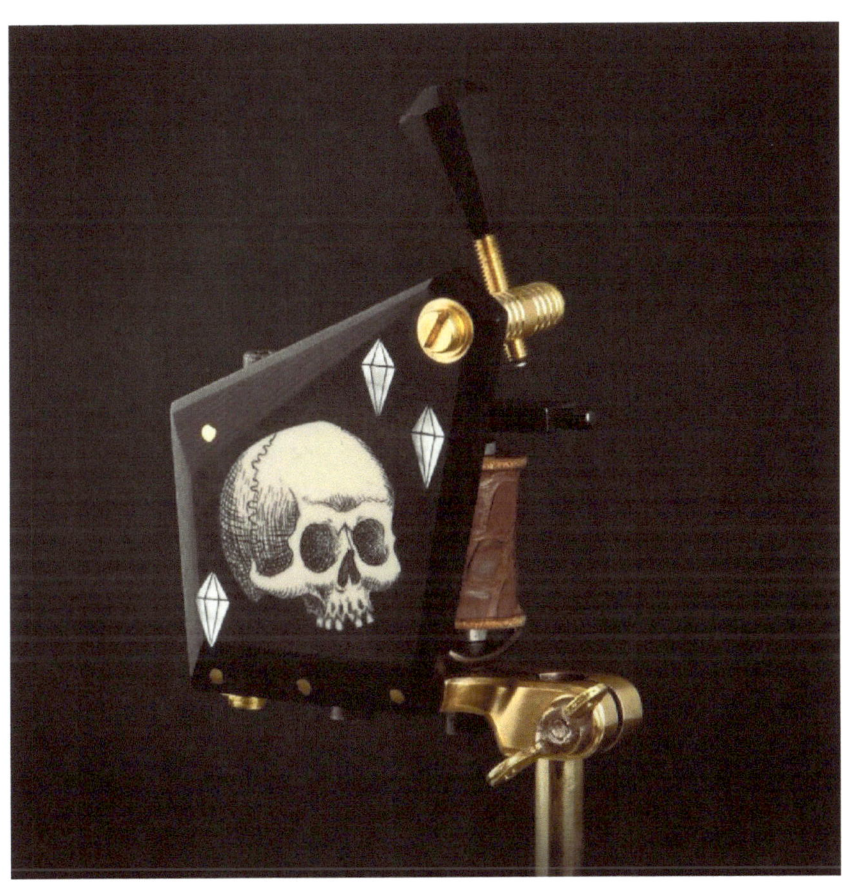

Cory Rogers and Soba

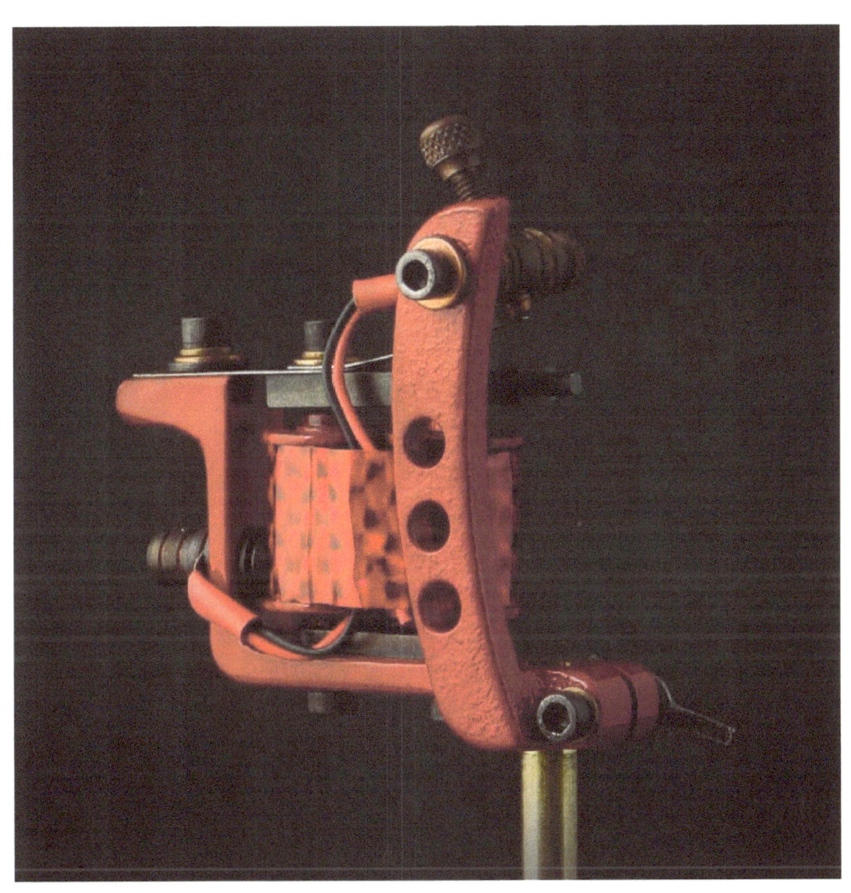

Bryce Stucke and Sebastian Lutz

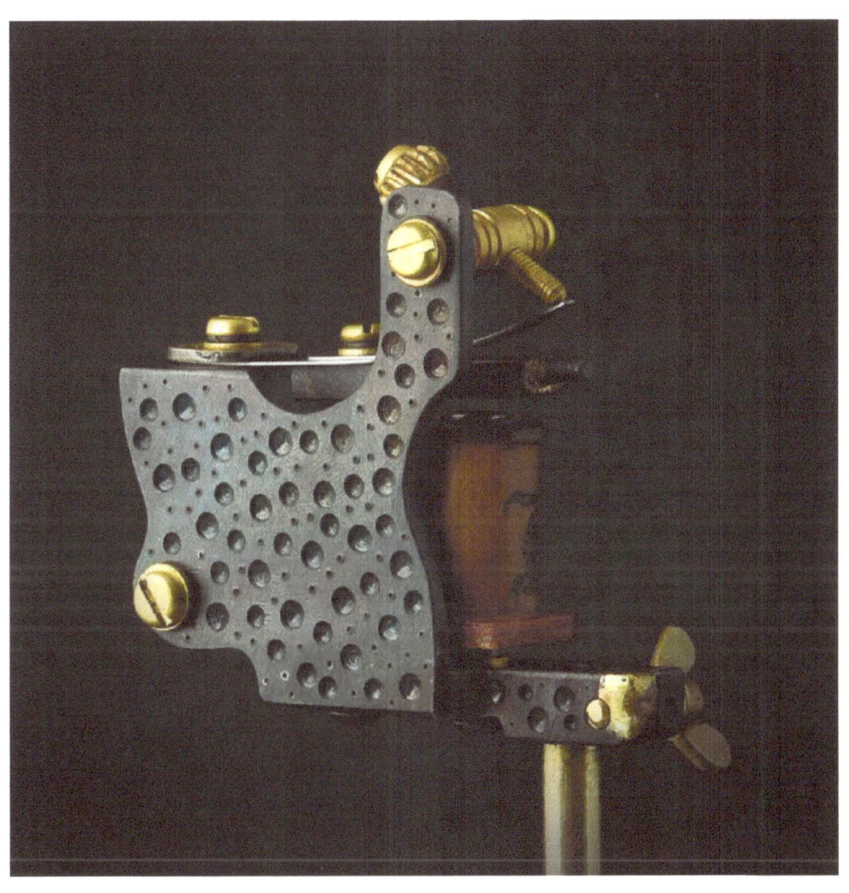

Dennis El Hombre Invisible and Salva

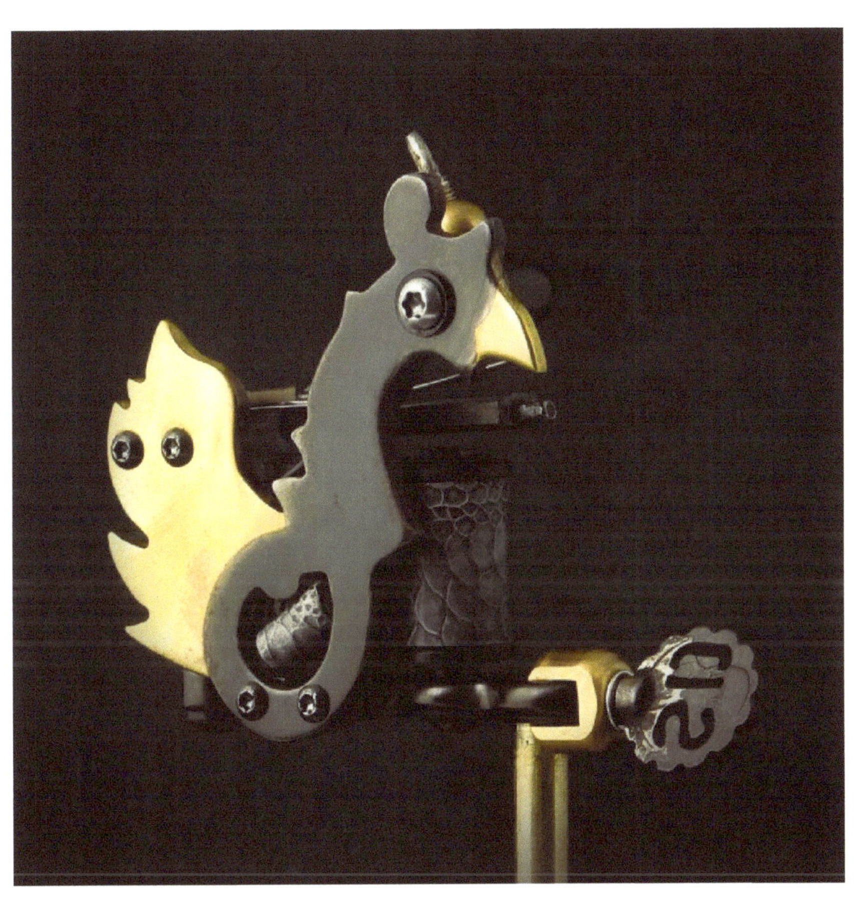

Joseph Mc Veigh and Todd Hlavaty

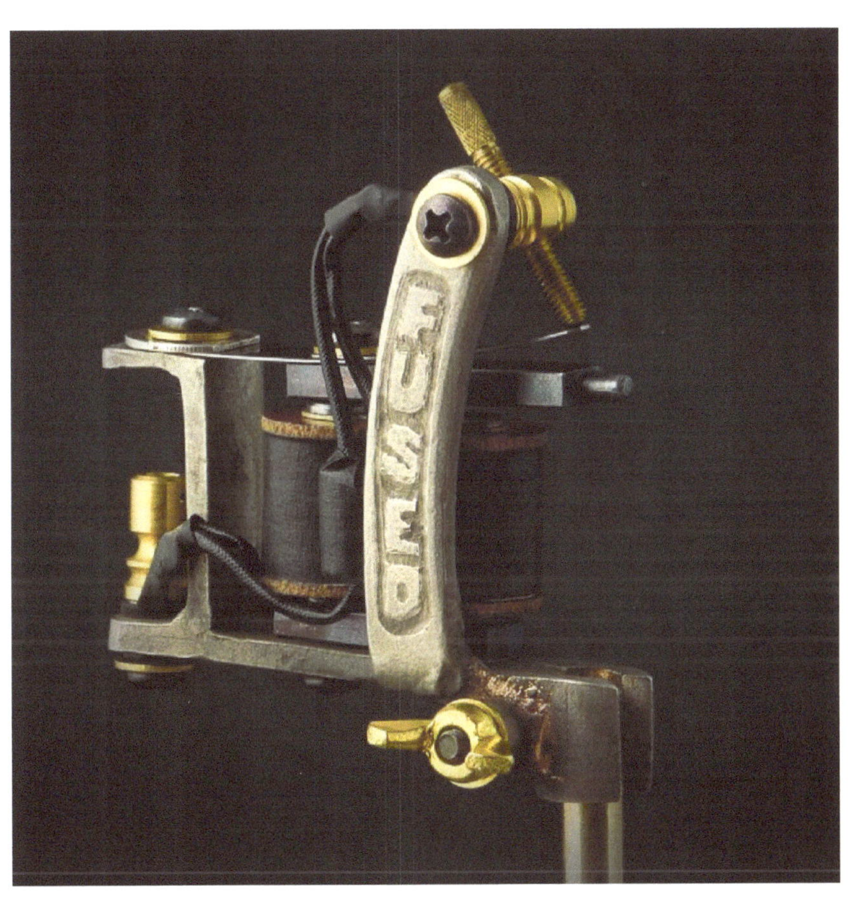

Chris Bonobo and Bruno Kea

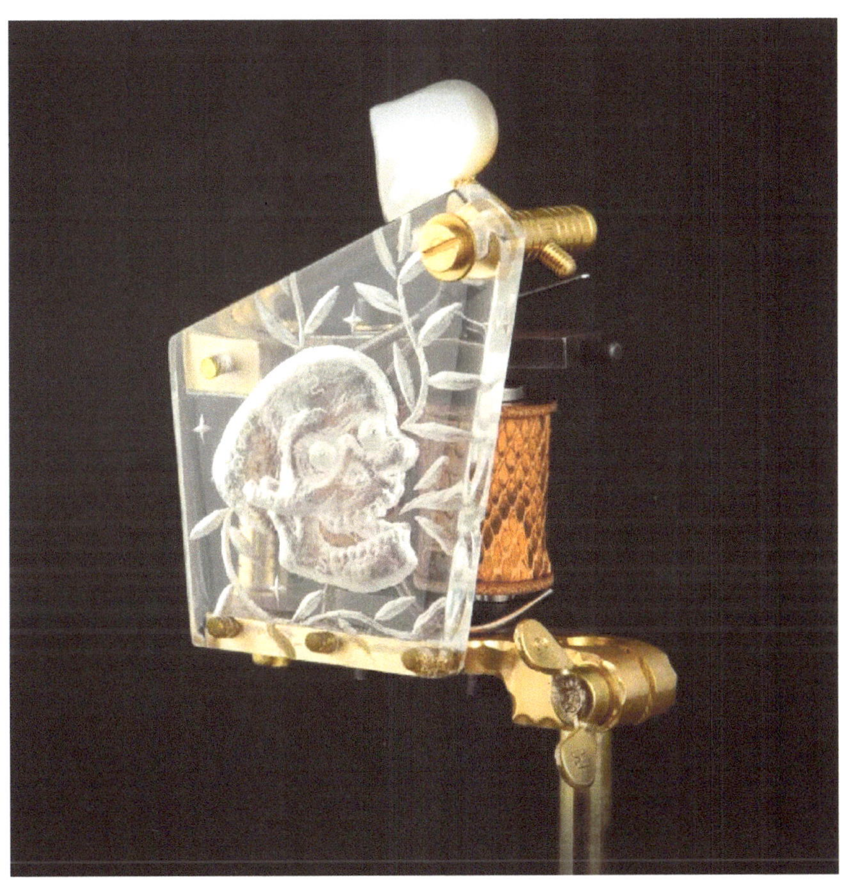

Greg DiGiacinto and Dirk Mellott

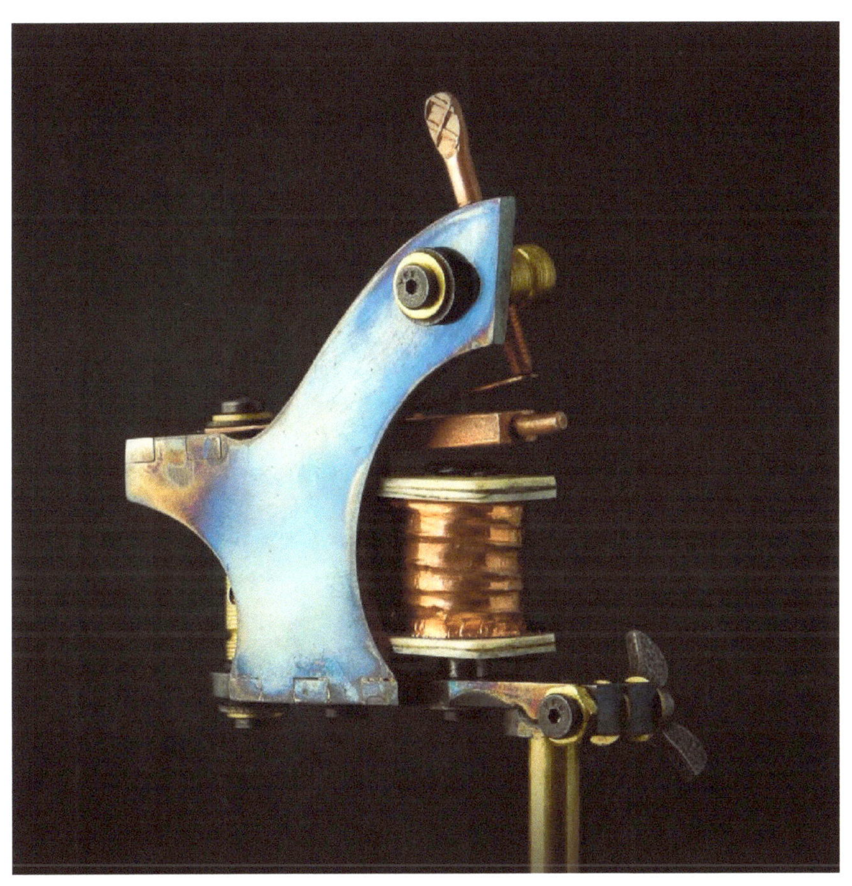

Andy Bolin
Austin Riley
Brian Fuentes
BR Irons
Bruno Kea
Bryce Stucke
Charles Freeland
Chris Bonobo
Chunk
Cory Rogers
Chris Quidgeon
Dan Dringenberg
Dan Labonté
Dano Collins
Dennis El Ombre Invisible
Dirk Mellott
Dr. Blood
Gregory DiGiacinto
Henry Rodriguez
Iko
Jay Addictive
Jason Haney
Jimmy Whitlock
John Clark
Jon Ondo

Joseph Mc Veigh
Karl Marc
Kris Cunningham
Marv Lerning Esquire
Mike Hendrix
Mike Palombo
Mike Pike
Mike Young
Nick Ackman
Nicko
Patrick Chaudesaigues
Paulo Cruzes
Peter Bobek
Rex Hobbs
Rob Rutherford
Safwan
Salva
Sebastian Lutz
Soba
Steve Turner
T. Massari
Todd Hlavaty
Toma
Tomas Khajl

Our heartfelt thanks to all the builders, all the people who made this book possible, and especially to Mehdi BENBACHIR for his commitment and photographic excellence.

Patrick CHAUDESAIGUES & IKO

Delux Custom Editions - Reissue 2023
Dépot légal : avril 2023
Tous droits réservés

www.delux-custom-editions.fr

FusedTattooMachines.com